HAL•LEONARD
STRUMENTAL
PLAY-ALONG

AUDIO
ACCESS
INCLUDED

CLARINET

MANNHEIM STEAMROLLER
Christmas

Audio Arrangements by Peter Deneff

ISBN 978-1-4803-9706-4

HAL•LEONARD®
CORPORATION
7777 W. BLUEMOUND RD. P.O. BOX 13819 MILWAUKEE, WI 53213

In Australia Contact:
Hal Leonard Australia Pty. Ltd.
4 Lentara Court
Cheltenham, Victoria, 3192 Australia
Email: ausadmin@halleonard.com.au

Visit Hal Leonard Online at
www.halleonard.com

CONTENTS

BRING A TORCH, JEANETTE ISABELLA

CLARINET

17th Century French Provencal Carol
Arranged by CHIP DAVIS

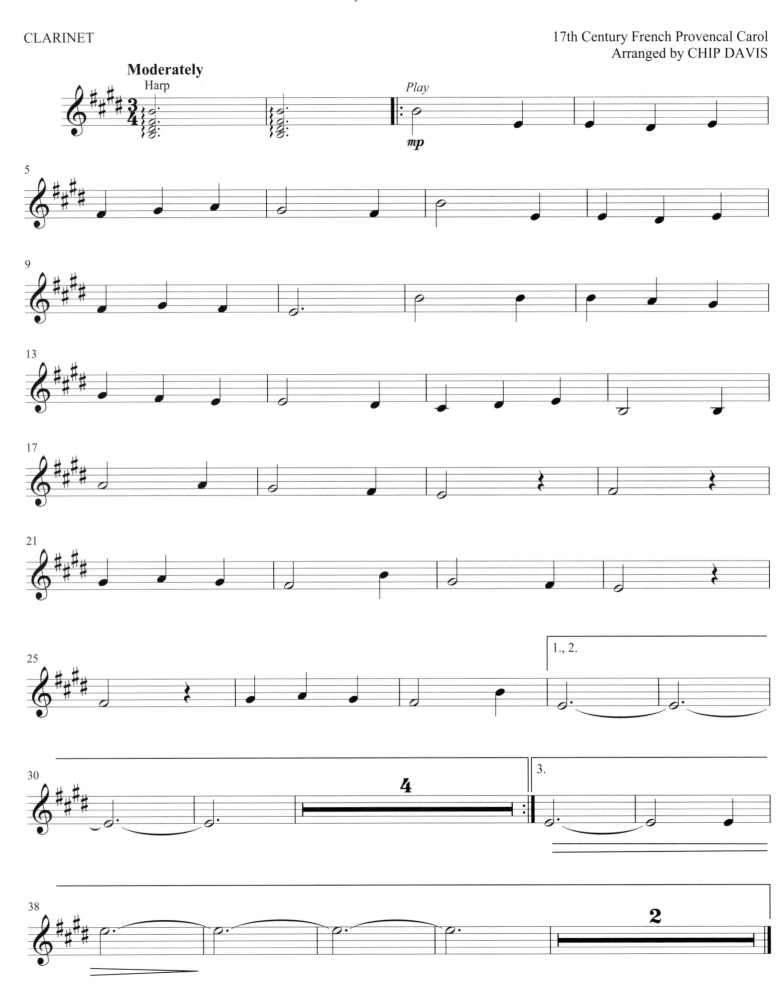

GOOD KING WENCESLAS

CLARINET

Arranged by CHIP DAVIS

CAROL OF THE BELLS

Ukrainian Christmas Carol
Arranged by CHIP DAVIS

CLARINET

CHRISTMAS LULLABY

CLARINET

By CHIP DAVIS

DECK THE HALLS

CLARINET

Arranged by CHIP DAVIS

GOD REST YE MERRY GENTLEMEN

CLARINET

19th Century English Carol
Arranged by CHIP DAVIS

GREENSLEEVES

CLARINET

Sixteenth Century Traditional English
Arranged by CHIP DAVIS

HARK! THE HERALD ANGELS SING

Clarinet

By FELIX MENDELSSOHN
Arranged by CHIP DAVIS

JOY TO THE WORLD

CLARINET

Arranged by CHIP DAVIS

PAT A PAN

Words and Music by BERNARD DE LA MONNOYE
Arranged by CHIP DAVIS

CLARINET